Presented to:

_____

From:

_____

Date:

_____

On the Occasion of:

_____

I pray that you ... may have power,
together with all the saints,
to grasp how wide and long
and high and deep is the love of Christ.

EPHESIANS 3:17-19

Lives of the Saints

Written by Bart Tesoriero

Illustrations by Michael Adams

Library of Congress Control Number: 2011940048
ISBN 1-936020-98-0

SAINTS IN ALPHABETICAL ORDER

SAINTS BY FEAST DAY

St. Elizabeth Ann Seton	January 4
St. John Neumann	January 5
St. Sebastian	January 20
St. Francis de Sales	January 24
St. Thomas Aquinas	January 28
St. Blaise	February 3
St. Apollonia	February 9
St. John of God	March 8
St. Louise de Marillac	March 15
St. Patrick	March 17
St. Joseph	March 19
St. Isidore of Seville	April 4
St. Vincent Ferrer	April 5
St. John Baptist de la Salle	April 7
St. Bernadette Soubirous	April 16
St. Catherine of Siena	April 29
St. Florian	May 4
St. Peregrine	May 4
St. Dymphna	May 15
St. Isidore the Farmer	May 15
St. Bernardine of Siena	May 20
St. Rita	May 22
St. Joan of Arc	May 30
St. Anthony	June 13
St. Thomas More	June 22
St. Paul	June 29
St. Peter the Apostle	June 29
St. Benedict	July 11
St. Veronica	July 12
St. Kateri Tekakwitha	July 14
St. Christopher	July 25
St. Anne	July 26
St. Martha	July 29
St. Ignatius of Loyola	July 31
St. John Vianney	August 4
St. Maximilian Kolbe	August 14
St. Roch	August 16
St. Rose of Lima	August 23
St. Augustine	August 28
The Blessed Virgin Mary	September 8
St. Adrian of Nicomedia	September 8
St. Matthew the Apostle	September 21
St. Pio of Pietrelcina	September 23
St. Vincent de Paul	September 27
St. Gabriel the Archangel	September 29
St. Michael the Archangel	September 29
St. Therese of Lisieux	October 1
St. Francis of Assisi	October 4
St. Teresa of Avila	October 15
St. Gerard	October 16
St. Luke the Evangelist	October 18
St. Martin de Porres	November 3
St. Charles Borromeo	November 4
St. Cecilia	November 22
St. Catherine of Alexandria	November 25
St. Francis Xavier	December 3
St. Barbara	December 4
St. Nicholas	December 6
St. Lucy	December 13
St. John the Apostle	December 27

FOREWORD

My dad used to tell my sisters and me, "God put you on this earth for only one reason: to get to heaven. If you miss that, you've missed everything." In his rather direct style, he got the point across, as did Blessed John Paul II: "You are **all** called to holiness!"

My dear young readers, God loves you ... and has for a very long time! God really wants a relationship with you. He wants you to be His friend. He sent His Son Jesus to live for you, die for you, and rise for you, so you could become His child and come to know Him better on earth, and then live in heaven with Him forever.

Saints are people who received God's love and who tried to return His love with all their hearts. On earth, they lived holy lives, serving God and their neighbors. They obeyed God and tried to help others. Now they are in heaven. The Church gives us the saints as our heroes of the faith. The Church calls us to follow their example—to imitate them as they imitated Jesus.

In this book, you will read the stories of some of the most well-beloved saints of our Church. You will meet holy people of the distant past, like Saint Anne, the grandmother of Jesus, as well as those of the present, like Saint Pio of Pietrelcina, who died less than 50 years ago. You will learn about angels and apostles, monks and martyrs, pastors and preachers, nuns and nurses, farmers and fishermen, and many more!

The Church gives us saints to help us follow Jesus with all our hearts, and to become all He has dreamed for us to be!

WHAT IS A SAINT?

God loves you! God loves each person He has ever created, from all eternity. A saint is someone who **knows and believes** that God loves him or her very much. They know that God loves them for who they are, and that He will never leave them or forsake them. A saint knows that Jesus gave His life to save us from our sins, and to make us holy, because He loves us.

Saints want to love God because He has first loved us. They give God permission to change them, to make them holy. Saints spend time with God in prayer. They receive the sacraments, especially Holy Communion, often. Because they feel the love of Jesus in their hearts, saints go all out for God. They seek to follow Him always.

Jesus taught us that the two greatest commandments are, "You shall love the Lord your God with all your heart, with all your soul, with all your mind, and with all your strength, and you shall love your neighbor as yourself." Saints obey God. They do what He tells us to do! A saint loves God with all of his or her heart. Saints love others as they love themselves. Jesus told us that there are no greater commandments than these.

Many of the saints were martyrs. A martyr is someone who gives witness to Jesus by dying for his or her faith. As you will read, many of the first saints gave their lives during the persecutions in the early centuries of the Church.

Finally, a saint is a hero of our faith. Saints lived what Saint Ignatius of Loyola prayed: "Dear Lord, teach us to give and not to count the cost. Amen."

SAINT ELIZABETH ANN SETON

Feast Day: January 4
Patron of Converts

Elizabeth Bayley was born in 1774 into an Episcopalian family. Her early life was quiet, simple, and often lonely. She loved to read the Bible and found great comfort in God's Word. Elizabeth married William Seton, but he died at an early age and left her with their five children. Elizabeth felt herself drawn to Christ in the Holy Eucharist, and she became a Roman Catholic in 1805. She founded the Sisters of Charity, beginning the American parochial school system. Mother Seton died in 1821, and became the first native-born American to be canonized!

Prayer to Saint Elizabeth Ann Seton for Converts

Dear Saint Elizabeth Ann Seton, you were a wife, a mother, a teacher, and the founder of a religious order. You became a Catholic because of your great love for Jesus in the most Blessed Sacrament. Please bless all of us who seek to know God as Catholics. Help us in our journey to a deeper faith, hope, and love. Dear God, through the prayers of Saint Elizabeth, give us all the grace to love You more, and to serve You with joy. In Jesus' name. Amen.

Saint Elizabeth Ann Seton, pray for us.

SAINT JOHN NEUMANN

Feast Day: January 5
Patron of Catholic Education

Saint John Neumann was born in Bohemia in 1811. He left his home and traveled across the ocean to New York, where he was ordained a priest. Because there were so few priests in America, Father Neumann cared for 200,000 Catholics! He traveled from village to village, walking roads and climbing mountains to visit the sick, teach children, and celebrate Mass. Father Neumann joined the Redemptorists, a congregation dedicated to helping the poor and most abandoned. In 1852, he was ordained Bishop of Philadelphia. Bishop Neumann organized the first Catholic school system in the United States. He died in 1860. In 1977, Saint John Neumann became the first American bishop to be canonized!

Prayer to Saint John Neumann

O Saint John Neumann, you left your home and country to serve God. Please pray for all who teach others about the Catholic faith. Dear God, through the prayers of Saint John Neumann, help us also to serve those who are poor and suffering. Help us to be true to Jesus even when it is hard. In Jesus' name. Amen.

Saint John Neumann, pray for us.

SAINT SEBASTIAN

Feast Day: January 20
Patron of Athletes

Saint Sebastian was born in Rome in the third century. Because of his noble birth and his bravery, the Emperor Diocletian made Sebastian a captain of his Imperial Guard.

Secretly a Christian, Sebastian healed the sick and led many to the Faith. When the emperor learned this, he ordered his soldiers to shoot Sebastian with arrows. By God's grace and because of his own physical fitness, Sebastian survived. For this reason, he is remembered today as the patron of athletes.

The emperor was very angry when he heard that Sebastian was still alive, and he ordered his soldiers to club him to death. Saint Sebastian died a true soldier for Jesus Christ.

Prayer to Saint Sebastian for Athletes

Glorious Saint Sebastian, although you were shot with arrows and left for dead, you survived because God helped you and you were so strong. You kept your faith in Christ even when the soldiers beat you, because you were so strong in your spirit. Therefore you won the prize of eternal life. Please ask God to bless all athletes. Help them and all of us to love Our Lord Jesus with all our hearts, souls, minds, and strength. Amen.

Saint Sebastian, pray for us.

SAINT FRANCIS DE SALES

Feast Day: January 24
Patron of Writers and Journalists

Saint Francis was born to a noble French family in 1567. He loved studies, and he earned doctorates from the University of Padua in both canon and civil law. Even more than studies, Francis loved God, because he knew that God loved him. He became a priest in 1593, and later became the bishop of Geneva. Saint Francis de Sales preached and wrote with great zeal. Through leaflets and books he had written, many people returned to the Church, and many faithful remained. As a result, Francis is remembered today as the patron of writers and the Catholic press.

Saint Francis de Sales died in 1622 and was canonized in 1653. In 1877, he was declared a Doctor of the Church.

Prayer to Saint Francis de Sales for Writers

Dear Saint Francis, out of your great love for God, you allowed yourself to be used as the instrument of His Word. Help all writers and journalists to copy your holy example of giving yourself to God. Dear God, through the prayers of Saint Francis de Sales, help all of us to think well, write well, and love well. In Jesus' name we pray. Amen.

Saint Francis de Sales, pray for us.

THOMAS ✦ AQUINAS ✦

SAINT THOMAS AQUINAS

Feast Day: January 28
Patron of Students

Saint Thomas Aquinas was born into a noble Italian family around 1226. When he was 17, he joined the Dominican Order, against his family's wishes. His brothers kidnapped him and held him prisoner for two years in their castle. However, Thomas escaped and went to Germany to study under Saint Albert the Great. He became a priest and was sent to the University of Paris, where he taught philosophy and theology for many years.

Saint Thomas deeply loved Our Lord Jesus. He wrote special prayers and hymns about the Blessed Sacrament. He wrote many books to help Christians understand more about Jesus and our faith. Saint Thomas Aquinas died in 1274. He was named one of the 33 Doctors, or Teachers, of the Church.

Prayer to Saint Thomas Aquinas for Students

Dear Saint Thomas Aquinas, please pray for all students. Help them to study well about God and all He has created. Help them to love wisdom and truth. Through your prayers, may God's light shine on us all. Amen.

Saint Thomas Aquinas, pray for us.

SAINT BLAISE

Feast Day: February 3
Patron of Veterinarians

According to legend, Blaise was born into a wealthy Christian family and trained as a doctor. He was ordained a bishop at a young age and he escaped the persecution of Diocletian by retiring to the hills and living as a hermit. In the wilderness, wild animals would come to him for healing and gather around his cave. Blaise would walk among them unafraid. One day the huntsmen of the Roman governor saw the wild animals gathered outside his cave and investigated. Discovering the bishop, they brought him before the governor, who tortured Blaise, but to no avail. Steadfast to the end, Blaise was finally beheaded around the year 316. Because he cared so well for animals, Saint Blaise is remembered today as the patron of veterinarians.

Prayer to Saint Blaise for Veterinarians

Dear Saint Blaise, please bless all veterinarians who work with animals. Help them to know the best ways of treating all the animals they see every day and comforting their owners. Help them to be as tender as you were with the wild animals and as firm as you were in the defense of the Faith. Amen.

Saint Blaise, pray for us.

SAINT APOLLONIA

Feast Day: February 9
Patron of Dentists

Saint Apollonia was born in Egypt. She preached the word of God all her life and risked persecution for her faith. In the year 249, Saint Apollonia was arrested. She told the judge, "I am a Christian and I love and serve the true God." He became very angry and tortured Apollonia. She stood firm and refused to deny Christ even when her persecutors smashed her teeth and knocked them out of her mouth. They threatened to burn her to death unless she denied Jesus. Rather than renounce her faith in Christ, Apollonia threw herself into the raging fire where she perished. When the pagans saw her heroism, many were converted.

Today, Saint Apollonia is recognized as the patron of dentists.

Prayer to Saint Apollonia for Dentists

Dear Saint Apollonia, you comforted many people during your life. By suffering the loss of your teeth and not fearing the fire meant to extinguish your faith, you won the crown of martyrdom and eternal happiness. Please bless all who work in dentistry. Help them to comfort and heal others. Amen.

Saint Apollonia, pray for us.

SAINT JOHN OF GOD

Feast Day: March 8
Patron of Printers and Publishers

Saint John of God was born in 1495 in Portugal. He left home as a young boy, but soon fell ill and was abandoned. A shepherd found John and cared for him. Then John left to become a soldier. As a soldier he did many things he would later regret.

One day John heard Saint John of Avila preach a sermon. John became aware of his sins and realized he needed to repent and return to God. He started his own hospital for all the poor and sick. He died in 1550 after ten years of service and was canonized in 1690.

Prayer to Saint John of God for Printers and Publishers

Dear Saint John, when you realized your sins had hurt God and others, you repented of them. You changed your life and set a new path for yourself. Through your many loving deeds, you revealed God's compassion and drew countless people to Him. Dear God, through the prayers of Saint John, bless all who work in printing and publishing. Help them to share Your love with others and to help people live good lives. In Jesus' name we pray. Amen.

Saint John of God, pray for us.

SAINT LOUISE DE MARILLAC

Feast Day: March 15

Patron of Nurses and Social Workers

Saint Louise de Marillac was born in 1591 in Paris, France. Her mother died after her birth. In 1613, she married, and she and her husband, Antoine, bore a son. In 1625, after a long illness, Antoine died. While raising her son, Louise did many good works. Saint Francis de Sales became her confessor and spiritual director. Through Saint Francis, Louise met Saint Vincent de Paul. In 1633, they began together the Daughters of Charity. The women who served in this order cared for the homeless poor and for the needy children who lived in the streets.

Until her death in 1660, Saint Louise worked with all her might for the poor. She also helped her country to improve its social services for the poor. Today, Saint Louise de Marillac is recognized as the patron of social workers.

Prayer to Saint Louise for Nurses and Social Workers

Dear Saint Louise, you endured trials and challenges in your life, yet you used your talents to transform every one of them into a beautiful work for God. Please pray for all nurses and social workers, that they might feel Our Lord's great love in their hearts and then reach out to serve His children. Amen.

Saint Louise de Marillac, pray for us.

SAINT PATRICK

Feast Day: March 17
Patron of Ireland and of Engineers

Saint Patrick was born around 389. At the age of 16, he was captured by pirates who took him to Ireland. Patrick stayed close to Jesus and the Catholic Faith. Six years later he escaped, and after many trials made his way home.

Patrick saw in a dream all the children of Ireland stretching out their hands from the wombs of their mothers, and crying to him. God showed Patrick that he was to return to Ireland and tell the people about Jesus.

Patrick returned to Ireland where he was made Bishop, and he traveled all over Ireland bringing the Faith. He restored sight to the blind, health to the sick, and raised the dead to life. He died on March 17 in the year 461.

Prayer to Saint Patrick for Ireland and Engineers

Dear Saint Patrick, you preached the good news of Jesus to the people of Ireland. You built many churches and monasteries. Please bless all engineers and help them to build good things for others. Help all of us to love one another and to trust Christ as you did. Amen!

Saint Patrick, pray for us.

SAINT JOSEPH

Feast Day: March 19

Patron of Fathers, Carpenters, and Homesellers

Saint Joseph was a young carpenter from the town of Nazareth. He was engaged to Mary. Before he and Mary lived together, the Angel Gabriel appeared to Mary and told her that God had chosen her to be the mother of His son. An angel also told Joseph, "Do not be afraid to take Mary as your wife. You are to name her child Jesus." Joseph awoke and did all the angel had told him to do.

After Jesus was born in Bethlehem, an angel spoke to Joseph in a dream, "Get up, take the child and his mother, and flee to Egypt! Stay there until I tell you." Joseph arose quickly and took Jesus and Mary to Egypt. Later they returned to Nazareth, where Joseph worked hard to take care of Mary and Jesus, whom he loved.

Prayer to Saint Joseph for Fathers and Workers

Dear Saint Joseph, you trusted in God and obeyed His commands. Help all fathers to love their families. Help all carpenters to build good homes. Please help homesellers to find good homes for people. O Saint Joseph, I love you! Thank you for being my friend and helper forever. Amen.

Saint Joseph, pray for us.

SAINT ISIDORE OF SEVILLE

Feast Day: April 4

Patron of the Internet and Computer Technicians

Isidore was born of a royal family in Spain in 560. He didn't get very good grades, so he ran away from school. He stopped for a drink of water from a spring, and noticed a stone, which was hollowed out by the dripping water. He realized that if he kept working at it, little by little, just like that dripping water, he could do great things. He returned to school, and by hard work he became a great bishop and teacher of the Faith.

Saint Isidore wrote 20 books which make up the first Christian Encyclopedia. Because of his ability to help people understand facts, Saint Isidore is the patron saint of the Internet and of computer technicians and programmers. Saint Isidore died on April 4, 636.

Prayer to Saint Isidore for Computer Technicians

O Saint Isidore, your love for God led you to study the Book of Nature and to preserve the wisdom of the whole world. Inspire those who work as computer technicians to use their skills to help us grow in true wisdom and service. Amen.

Saint Isidore, pray for us.

SAINT VINCENT FERRER

Feast Day: April 5

Patron of Plumbers

Saint Vincent Ferrer was born on January 23, 1350, in Valencia, Spain. His father dreamed that Vincent would grow up to be a famous friar. At 18, Vincent joined the Dominicans. After much study, he became a master of sacred theology. He loved and memorized God's Word as well.

In 1398, Vincent became very sick from sadness, since the Church was divided by a Great Schism. Our Lord Jesus appeared to Vincent in a vision and healed him. He told Vincent to preach and tell everyone to repent and be holy. For the next 21 years, he preached and worked stupendous miracles throughout Europe, converting thousands of people.

Saint Vincent was so successful at building up the Church that today he is remembered as the patron of the building trades and of plumbers in particular. He died in 1419.

Prayer to Saint Vincent Ferrer for Plumbers

Dear Saint Vincent, by opening yourself up to God, you allowed His grace to flow into the lives of many. Dear God, through the prayers of Saint Vincent, bless all plumbers, and all who build up Your Church. In Jesus' name. Amen.

Saint Vincent Ferrer, pray for us.

SAINT JOHN BAPTIST DE LA SALLE

Feast Day: April 7
Patron of Teachers

Saint John Baptist de la Salle was born in 1651 in France. He decided to follow Jesus at an early age, and became a priest in 1678. John wanted to help children learn better. In 1679, he helped a friend open up a school for poor boys. He realized that was what he wanted to do the rest of his life.

Saint John believed that the best way to serve his students was to teach their teachers. He therefore established the Institute of the Brothers of the Christian Schools in 1680. Soon after, he founded colleges for training teachers. John died in 1719, but his work spread quickly throughout the whole world. Pope Leo XIII canonized Saint John Baptist de la Salle in 1900, and in 1950 he was made the patron saint of teachers.

Prayer to Saint John Baptist de la Salle for Teachers

Dear Saint John Baptist de la Salle, you gave your life to educating the poorest members of the Church. Pray for all teachers to see Christ in their students and to live always for Him. Dear God, through the prayers of Saint John, please give Your Church good teachers today. In Jesus' name we pray. Amen.

Saint John Baptist de la Salle, pray for us.

SAINT BERNADETTE SOUBIROUS

Feast Day: April 16

Patron of the Sick

Bernadette Soubirous was born in Lourdes, France, in 1844. One day, as she was gathering firewood beside a river, Bernadette saw a beautiful Lady wearing a blue and white dress who was floating above a rose bush. The Lady smiled at her and made the Sign of the Cross with a golden rosary. Bernadette knelt down and began to pray. The Lady, who was the Virgin Mary, asked Bernadette to dig nearby. When she did so, a spring emerged with healing waters. Mary asked Bernadette to have a chapel built by the spot, so people could come there to wash and drink. The water from this spring continues to bring healings to many people. Our Lady also requested that a church be built there. Bernadette became a nun, and died a few years later. Pope Pius XI canonized Saint Bernadette in 1933.

Prayer to Saint Bernadette

Dear Saint Bernadette, thank you for being true to Mary, the Lady whom you saw, and to Jesus, her Son. Please pray for all who are ill or suffering. Dear God, through the prayers of Mother Mary and dear Saint Bernadette, please heal the sick in body and soul. In Jesus' name. Amen.

Saint Bernadette, pray for us.

SAINT CATHERINE OF SIENA

Feast Day: April 29
Patron of Nurses

Saint Catherine of Siena was born on March 25, 1347, in Siena, Italy. As a young girl, she had visions of angels. At the age of 15, Catherine entered the Third Order of Saint Dominic. She loved to pray quietly alone with God, and then serve others with love and joy. Catherine traveled through Italy, bringing people back to obedience to the Pope, and winning hardened souls to God.

Saint Catherine died at the age of 33. In 1970, Pope Paul VI declared Saint Catherine of Siena and Saint Teresa of Avila to be the first women Doctors, or Teachers, of the Church.

Prayer to Saint Catherine of Siena for Nurses

Dear Saint Catherine, because of your devotion to Jesus, God used you to bring healing to the world. Lord God, through the prayers of Saint Catherine of Siena, please bless all nurses. Heal every person who is in their care. May their loving attention and kindness help draw their patients to You. In Jesus' name we pray. Amen.

Saint Catherine of Siena, pray for us.

SAINT FLORIAN

Feast Day: May 4
Patron of Firefighters

Florian was born around 250 A.D. He was a commander of the Roman Imperial Army. He was also secretly a Christian, who helped to organize firefighting brigades. According to an old story, Florian once stopped a town from burning by praying and throwing a single bucket of water on the blaze.

One day, Florian was ordered to put some Christians to death. He refused, and admitted that he was proud to be a follower of Jesus. The other soldiers beat and tortured him with clubs, spikes, and fire. Then they tied a stone around his neck and drowned him.

Saint Florian was martyred around 304 A.D. He is remembered today as the patron of firefighters.

Prayer to Saint Florian for Firefighters

Dear Saint Florian, your love for Christ burned brighter than the flames with which you were tortured. Protect all who serve as firefighters and give them a deep desire to follow Our Lord as you did. Dear God, please bless all who serve as firefighters. Keep them safe and strong. In Jesus' name. Amen.

Saint Florian, pray for us.

SAINT PEREGRINE

Feast Day: May 4

Patron of Cancer Patients

Saint Peregrine was born in 1260 in Italy. He enjoyed many fine pleasures and riches. At the age of 30, he accepted Jesus as his Lord, was baptized, and gave his life to God. Saint Peregrine became a priest in an order of men called the Servants of Mary, or the Servites. He spent his life caring for the sick, the poor, and the forgotten. At the age of 60, he was diagnosed with a severe cancer in his leg.

The night before his leg was to be amputated, Peregrine dragged himself before the crucifix and begged Jesus to heal him. In a vision, he saw Jesus lean down from the Cross to touch and heal his leg. Saint Peregrine died on May 1, 1345, and was canonized on December 27, 1726.

Prayer to Saint Peregrine for Cancer Patients

O great Saint Peregrine, in a vision you saw Jesus coming down from His Cross to heal you. Please ask God to bless and heal all those who suffer from cancer and skin disease. May He also bless their families and those who care for them. In Jesus' name. Amen.

Saint Peregrine, pray for us.

SAINT DYMPHNA

Feast Day: May 15
Patron of Counselors and Psychologists

Saint Dymphna was born in Ireland to a pagan chief named Damon and a Christian mother. When Dymphna was 14, her beloved mother died. Her father became mentally ill with sadness. His evil counselors told him to take his daughter as a wife. Saint Dymphna fled to Belgium, but her father found her and told her to return to Ireland as his bride. When she refused, he drew his sword and struck off her head. Saint Dymphna was martyred around 620 A.D. Many sick people have been healed at her shrine, built on the spot where she was buried. Saint Dymphna is the patron of counselors.

Prayer to Saint Dymphna for Counselors

Dear Saint Dymphna, through your prayers many people have been healed of mental illness. Please help and bless all counselors. Help them to bring healing, comfort, and compassion to the confused and the sick in their care.

Lord God, through the prayers of Saint Dymphna, pour out Your Spirit of wisdom and good counsel on all who advise others, that they may always glorify You and lead all Your children to You. In Jesus' name. Amen.

Saint Dymphna, pray for us.

SAINT ISIDORE THE FARMER

Feast Day: May 15
Patron of Farmers and Farm Workers

Isidore was born in Madrid, Spain, around the year 1070. He rose up early every morning to go to Mass. Then he would go to work in the fields. One day some farm workers complained that Isidore was always late for work. When the master investigated, he found that an angel plowed the field while Isidore prayed.

Isidore married Maria Torribia, who is also a canonized saint. The couple had one son, but he died in his youth. Isidore died on May 15, 1130. Many miracles and cures are reported at his grave. Today, Saint Isidore is venerated as the patron of farmers.

Prayer to Saint Isidore for Farmers

Dear Saint Isidore, you let the seed of the Gospel take root in you and produce good fruit. Please pray that we will allow Jesus to live in us as you did. Dear God, through the prayers of Saint Isidore, please bless all farmers and farm laborers to love You and serve others. Please keep them safe and protect them. Supply their needs, as they supply food for us. In Jesus' name. Amen.

Saint Isidore the Farmer, pray for us.

SAINT BERNARDINE OF SIENA

Feast Day: May 20
Patron of Advertisers

Saint Bernardine was born in 1380 in Siena, Italy. He joined the Franciscans in 1402 and was ordained two years later. His voice was very weak because of an illness. Through the prayers of Our Mother Mary, he was healed and began preaching.

When preaching, Saint Bernardine would often hold up a card with the name of Jesus. He urged people to turn to Our Lord and accept His grace. Saint Bernardine preached for the rest of his life and died in 1444.

Saint Bernardine was canonized a saint in 1450. He is the patron of advertisers because he was very gifted at persuading people to love God and do good.

Prayer to Saint Bernardine of Siena for Advertisers

Saint Bernardine, through your preaching, thousands of people returned to God. Help all people who work as advertisers to be wise and good. Dear God, through the prayers of Saint Bernadine, please help advertisers to use their skills for Your glory and the good of others. Help all of us to be Your witnesses in all we do and say. In Jesus' name. Amen.

Saint Bernardine of Siena, pray for us.

SAINT RITA

Feast Day: May 22

Patron of Parents

Saint Rita was born in Italy in 1381. She wanted to become a nun, but her parents arranged for her to marry a man named Mancini. Rita obediently married him and gave birth to two sons. 18 years passed and Mancini was stabbed to death by an enemy. Rita prayed for him and he gave his soul to Jesus before he died. Her sons also died, and Rita became a nun. She lived 40 years in the convent, in great prayer and charity, working for peace in the area.

Rita loved Jesus very much. One day her forehead was miraculously pierced by a thorn from the Crown of Thorns. After suffering 15 years, Saint Rita died in 1457. Saint Rita loved her husband, her family, and her fellow sisters as a wife, a mother, a widow, and a nun.

Prayer to Saint Rita for Parents

Dear Saint Rita, please bless my Mom and Dad, and all parents. Help them to feel God's love in their hearts for one another and for us their children. Protect them through your prayers and help them to be happy together forever. Amen.

Saint Rita, pray for us.

SAINT JOAN OF ARC

Feast Day: May 30

Patron of France

Saint Joan of Arc was born in France in 1412. One day, as she cared for the sheep on her family farm, she heard the voices of some of the saints. They told Joan to help the king of France fight his enemies.

At the young age of 17, Joan went to help the king. She won the battle for Orleans, France, with a small army. She won many more battles, and helped the king to regain the throne of France.

The king's enemies kidnapped Joan and put her in prison. Joan was condemned to death because she refused to lie and say the saints had not spoken to her. She was burned at the stake on May 30, 1431, at the age of 19. However, the Church later canonized her as Saint Joan of Arc.

Prayer to Saint Joan of Arc

Dear Saint Joan of Arc, God gave you great skill in fighting for France. Through your prayers may He bless all women who love and stand up for their families, their country, and their Faith. In Jesus' name. Amen.

Saint Joan of Arc, pray for us.

SAINT ANTHONY

Feast Day: June 13

Patron of Lost Things and Missing Persons

Saint Anthony was born in Portugal in 1195 and became a Franciscan at the age of 26. God gave him the gift of preaching to touch the hearts of his listeners. When Saint Anthony spoke about Jesus and his Mother Mary, many people returned to Jesus and the Catholic faith. Saint Anthony asked Mary to help him when he preached, and God worked many miracles through him. One night, a friend saw a beautiful little Child standing upon a book, and clinging with both of His little arms around Anthony's neck. It was the Infant Jesus. Saint Anthony died at the age of 36, and the very next year he was canonized a saint.

Prayer to Saint Anthony to Find Lost Articles

Dear Saint Anthony, God has made you a powerful patron and helper to find lost or misplaced objects. We turn to you today with confidence and love. Through your prayer, may God help us to find what we have lost. Dear Saint Anthony, help us also be close to Jesus this day, and to always find Him in our hearts. Amen.

Saint Anthony, pray for us.

SAINT THOMAS MORE

Feast Day: June 22
Patron of Lawyers

Saint Thomas More was born in London in 1478. He studied law at Oxford University and was elected to Parliament. In 1501, Thomas became a lawyer and began his career as a civil servant. King Henry VIII appointed him as Lord Chancellor of England in 1529. Saint Thomas refused to honor the King as the Head of the Church of England and was confined to the Tower of London, where he was convicted of treason. Saint Thomas More was beheaded on July 6, 1535. He told the crowd, "I die as the King's good servant—but God's first!" Because of his honesty and fairness, Saint Thomas is recognized today as the patron of attorneys and lawyers.

Prayer to Saint Thomas More for Attorneys

Dear Saint Thomas, you dedicated your life to learning the truth. You served your king, but you served God first. Dear God, through the intercession of Saint Thomas More, please bless all lawyers and attorneys. Give them the courage to stand up for truth and justice, even if they must stand alone. Let them know You will never leave them nor forsake them. In Jesus' name. Amen.

Saint Thomas More, pray for us.

SAINT PAUL

Feast Day: June 29
Patron of Writers

Saint Paul was born as Saul of Tarsus to Jewish parents. He did not believe in Jesus and persecuted the Christians. He held the robes of those who stoned Saint Stephen, the first martyr in the early days of the Church. A martyr is someone who dies as a witness to their faith in Jesus.

One day, a brilliant light flashed around Saul. He fell to the ground and heard the voice of Jesus saying, "Saul, Saul, why are you persecuting Me?" Saul repented of his sins, was baptized, and changed his name to Paul.

Saint Paul preached the Gospel everywhere he went. He suffered much for Christ. Saint Paul was put into prison in Rome, where he was beheaded as a martyr.

Prayer to Saint Paul for Writers

Dear Saint Paul, you wrote many Letters to help your fellow Christians understand and follow Our Lord. Please bless all writers with the grace to inspire others with the words of truth and the fire of love. Amen.

Saint Paul, pray for us.

SAINT PETER THE APOSTLE

Feast Day: June 29

Patron of Fishermen

Saint Peter was from a town called Bethsaida near the Sea of Galilee. He and his brother Andrew were fishermen when they met Jesus. One day, Jesus told them, "Follow Me, and I will make you fishers of men." The two brothers left their boat and their father and followed Jesus.

Jesus said, "You are Peter, and on this rock I will build My Church." He then gave Peter the keys to the kingdom of heaven. Peter was our first Pope. After Jesus went back to heaven, Peter guided the Church as Jesus had told him.

Peter went to Rome to bring the Gospel to the whole world and to build up the Church. He wrote two Letters, known as Epistles. Saint Peter was crucified upside down by the Emperor Nero and buried on Vatican Hill.

Prayer to Saint Peter for Fishermen

Saint Peter, you left your nets upon the shore and followed Jesus. Please help all fishermen to do well and help all of us to lead others to Jesus by our words and actions. Amen.

Saint Peter, pray for us.

SAINT BENEDICT

Feast Day: July 11

Patron of Monks and Explorers

Saint Benedict was born in 480, to a noble Roman family. Because of the wickedness of the people, he left Rome and journeyed to a cave deep in a mountain. He lived alone there for three years. God gave Saint Benedict the power to work miracles. He spoke God's Word and saw visions of heaven. He served the poor and taught people about the Gospel. In time, other men came to stay with him. They formed the Benedictine Order of monks.

Saint Benedict and his monks moved to Monte Cassino. They built an Abbey, and there Saint Benedict wrote his rule for monastic life. His rule is simply: *Pray and Work.* Saint Benedict died at Monte Cassino with his hands lifted in prayer to the heavens, in the year 547.

Prayer to Saint Benedict for Monks and Explorers

Dear Saint Benedict, many men wanted to be around you because you were both holy and kind. Help all monks to be true to the Lord and to grow in love for all people. Bless also all those who explore new lands and new ways to help people become all that God wants them to be. Amen.

Saint Benedict, pray for us.

SAINT VERONICA

Feast Day: July 12
Patron of Photographers

According to tradition, Saint Veronica is the woman who wiped the face of Jesus with her veil as He carried the cross on His way to Calvary. The cloth was imprinted with the image of Jesus' face. The relic is still preserved in Saint Peter's Basilica, and the memory of Veronica's act of charity is commemorated in the Stations of the Cross.

It is unclear what happened to Saint Veronica after the Crucifixion. Some say she brought the image to Rome and miraculously healed the Emperor Tiberius of an ailment.

Because of the image that appeared on her veil, Saint Veronica is recognized today as the patron of photographers.

Prayer to Saint Veronica for Photographers

Dear Saint Veronica, you looked with pity on Jesus in His suffering. You offered Him your veil to wipe His face. In return for your great kindness, He left upon that cloth the imprint of His holy face. Help all photographers to see the face of Jesus in everyone they meet. Amen.

Saint Veronica, pray for us.

SAINT KATERI TEKAKWITHA

Feast Day: July 14

Patron of the Environment

Tekakwitha—*She who bumps into things*—was born to a Mohawk warrior and a Christian mother in New York in 1656. Her parents died in a smallpox epidemic that left her with weakened eyes and a scarred face. Tekakwitha was living with her uncle and aunt when the Jesuit priests—the "Blackrobes"—came to her village. She told them that she wanted to be a Christian, and on Easter Sunday, 1676, Kateri (Catherine) Tekakwitha was baptized. Kateri left her family and traveled many miles to Canada, where she found refuge at the Saint Francis Xavier Mission. Kateri cared tenderly for children, the sick, and the elderly. After a long illness, she died in 1680. Pope John Paul II beatified Kateri, and on October 21, 2012, Pope Benedict XVI canonized Kateri Tekakwitha, the first Native American to be declared a Saint!

Prayer to Saint Kateri Tekakwitha for our Earth

Dear Saint Kateri, you loved God and all His creation. Please pray that all people will care for our earth. May we use the gifts of our earth to bring glory to God and good to others, especially the poor and suffering. Amen.

Saint Kateri Tekakwitha, pray for us.

SAINT CHRISTOPHER

Feast Day: July 25

Patron of Travelers and Truck Drivers

Saint Christopher was a very strong man who lived long ago. He carried travelers on his back across a nearby river. One cold stormy night, a little Child knocked on the door of Christopher's cottage and asked him for a ride across the river. As they crossed the water, the Child grew heavier and heavier until Christopher thought they would both be swept away by the rushing stream. "Who are you?" he asked.

The Child answered, "I am Jesus, and I bear the world on my shoulders." Christopher knelt in worship and received his name, which means *Christ-Bearer*. After that night, he preached about Christ to all who came his way, and he died as a martyr for the Child. Saint Christopher is the patron of all travelers and truck drivers.

Prayer to Saint Christopher for Truck Drivers

Mighty Saint Christopher, you carried Jesus on your shoulders. Jesus carries us all on His shoulders. Please pray with us to God that He will help all truck drivers and travelers to be safe and alert. May they see Christ and serve Him in the people they meet along their way. Amen.

Saint Christopher, pray for us.

SAINT ANNE

Feast Day: July 26
Patron of Homemakers

Saint Anne was the mother of the Virgin Mary and the grandmother of Jesus. According to tradition, she and her husband, Saint Joachim, had prayed a long time to have a child. God answered their prayer and Anne gave birth to a beautiful little girl whom they named Mary.

Saints Joachim and Anne raised Mary to be a good girl. Saint Anne taught her to cook, to clean, to tend a garden, and most of all, to love God and serve Him.

Today, Saint Anne is remembered as the patron saint of homemakers because she was chosen by God to teach Mary how to be a good mother. Saint Anne and Saint Joachim, the grandparents of Jesus, share the same feast day.

Prayer to Saint Anne for Homemakers

Dear Saint Anne, help all our parents who try to make a happy and comfortable home for us. Please ask God to bless in a special way our mothers and grandmothers. Help all parents everywhere to make a home for Jesus in the hearts of their children. Amen.

Saint Anne, pray for us.

SAINT MARTHA

Feast Day: July 29
Patron of Cooks and Servers

Saint Martha lived in the town of Bethany with her sister Mary and her brother Lazarus. Jesus loved them and He liked to visit at their home with His apostles. Martha loved to cook and care for Jesus. Mary liked to sit at Jesus' feet and listen to Him speak. One day Martha was upset because Mary did not help her to cook and serve the food for Jesus and His friends. Jesus said to her, "Martha, Martha, you are worried about many things. Only one thing is necessary. Listen to Me."

Martha learned her lesson. Later on, when Lazarus died, Martha trusted Jesus to raise him from the dead. She is recognized today as the patron of all who cook, clean, and serve others with love.

Prayer to Saint Martha for Cooks and Servers

Dear Saint Martha, you received Jesus in your home and served Him at your table. Help all who serve others to do so with love, joy, and a cheerful heart. Help all of us to remember that in serving others, we are serving Our Lord. Amen.

Saint Martha, pray for us.

SAINT IGNATIUS OF LOYOLA

Feast Day: July 31
Patron of Educators and Retreatants

Saint Ignatius was born at Loyola, Spain, in the year 1491. After being wounded in battle, he decided to serve Jesus as his King. Ignatius went to study at the University of Paris, where several young men joined him to serve Christ. They were known as the "Companions of Jesus," or the Jesuits. "The Companions," said Ignatius, "are ready to do any work or go anywhere in the world for God's greater glory." They became famous teachers, and continued to serve the poor. The Jesuits lived and taught as soldiers of Christ.

Saint Ignatius suffered many trials, but he trusted in God, and composed his famous "Spiritual Exercises." Saint Ignatius died on July 31, 1556.

Prayer to Saint Ignatius of Loyola for Educators

Dear Saint Ignatius, you loved helping others to find Jesus in their hearts and souls. You loved learning because as we learn more about God, we are able to love Him more. Please pray for all teachers to help their students find God's truth and also His love. Amen.

Saint Ignatius, pray for us.

SAINT JOHN VIANNEY

Feast Day: August 4
Patron of Priests

Saint John Marie Vianney was born in France in 1786. He was ordained a priest in 1815 and sent to Ars, a little French village. He lived for his parishioners. He ate only a few potatoes and slept only a few hours every night, to win the graces of conversion for his parishioners. Thousands across the world came to him for Confession and healing. The devil tormented Father Vianney, waking him at night with mocking voices, loud noises and even physical abuse, but Saint John Vianney kept very close to Jesus and Mary. He was so holy and good that even very evil sinners were converted at his mere word. Saint John Vianney died in 1859, and his body did not decay, but lies incorrupt to this very day. Pope Benedict XVI declared him the patron of all priests in 2009.

Prayer to Saint John Vianney for Priests

Dear Saint John Vianney, you were devoted to God and His people. Lord God, through the prayers of Saint John Vianney, please bless all priests. Help them to be holy and true. May they be bold and loving witnesses to the truth, and draw many to You. In Jesus' name we pray. Amen.

Saint John Vianney, pray for us.

SAINT MAXIMILIAN KOLBE

Feast Day: August 14
Patron of Prisoners and Drug Addicts

Saint Maximilian Kolbe was born in 1894 in Poland and became a Franciscan priest. He founded the Immaculata Movement devoted to Our Lady. He used publications and a world-wide community to spread this devotion as far as Japan and India. In 1941, the Nazis arrested Father Kolbe and sent him to a prison camp in Auschwitz, Poland. A prisoner escaped, and the Nazis chose ten men to die as a warning to the others. Father Kolbe offered himself to die in the place of a young husband and father.

After two weeks without food or water, Father Kolbe was injected with acid, and died on August 14th, 1941. He is the patron of all those who struggle with addiction to drugs. In 1982 Pope John Paul II canonized Saint Maximilian Kolbe and declared him a martyr of love.

Prayer to Saint Maximilian Kolbe for Prisoners

Dear Saint Maximilian Kolbe, you loved others enough to die for them. Please help all who are in prison or who struggle with addiction to know the peace of God and the love of Mother Mary, who are always with them. Amen.

Saint Maximilian Kolbe, pray for us.

SAINT ROCH

Feast Day: August 16

Patron of All who Heal Contagious Diseases

Saint Roch was born with a red cross on his chest in the year 1295 in France. His parents died when he was a young man, and he joined the Third Order of Saint Francis. Roch cared for victims of the plague, a serious disease, in Rome. He healed many people by making the sign of the Cross over them. Then one day, Roch also became sick. He went into the forest to die, but a dog became his friend. The dog took food from his master's table, and brought it to Roch. In time, Roch got better!

Roch returned to town but was put into prison by mistake. An angel cared for him there until his death five years later. The day Roch died, his father came into his cell and recognized him by the cross on his chest. Saint Roch, or Rocco, was canonized 100 years after his death.

Prayer to Saint Roch for all who heal Contagious Diseases

Dear Saint Roch, God's power in you was so great that by the sign of the Cross, many people were healed of their diseases. Please heal those who are sick and suffering in our world and bless those who care for them. Amen.

Saint Roch, pray for us.

SAINT ROSE OF LIMA

Feast Day: August 23
Patron of Florists and Gardeners

Isabel Flores de Oliva was born in Lima, Peru, in 1586. She was so lovely that her parents called her Rose. Rose grew more beautiful and more in love with Jesus ever day.

Rose joined the Dominican Third Order in 1606, at age 20, and gave herself as a virgin to Christ. She lived alone in the family garden, raising vegetables and serving the poor and sick.

God gave Rose visions and blessings, and she also suffered in her body, soul, and spirit. God increased His love in her heart as she offered herself to Him. Saint Rose of Lima died at the age of 31 in 1617.

Prayer to Saint Rose of Lima

Dear Saint Rose, you loved God with all your heart, with all your body, and with all your mind. Please bless those who bring joy to others as florists and gardeners. Dear God, through the prayers of Saint Rose help us to please You always. In Jesus' name. Amen.

Saint Rose of Lima, pray for us.

SAINT AUGUSTINE

Feast Day: August 28

Patron of Theologians and Printers

Saint Augustine was born in 354, in Africa. He was smart and popular. However, his heart was far from God. His mother, Monica, prayed every day that God would help her son. After 33 years, God answered Saint Monica's prayers. Augustine asked Jesus to come into his heart, and God gave Augustine the gift of faith. He was baptized and gave all his goods to the poor. He became a bishop and fought the enemies of the Church by his life, preaching, and writing. "Our hearts are made for You, O Lord," he wrote, "and they are restless until they rest in You." Saint Augustine died in 430.

Prayer to Saint Augustine for Theologians and Printers

Dear Saint Augustine, you loved Jesus very much. You studied to know Jesus better, so that you could love Him more. Please bless all men and women who study about God. Through your prayers, may God help us to know Him better, to love Him more, and to serve Him with joy.

Please bless all who print books so others can learn about God and the amazing world He has created. Amen.

Saint Augustine, pray for us.

THE BLESSED VIRGIN MARY

Feast Day: September 8
Patron of Mothers

The Virgin Mary is the most lovely and loving of all God's creations. Through God's grace, Mary was conceived in her mother's womb without Original Sin. Mary in turn gave her whole self and life to God.

God sent the angel Gabriel to Mary when she was a young woman. Gabriel asked her if she would be willing to become the Mother of Jesus. Mary said, "Yes! Let it be done unto me according to thy word." Joseph took Mary as his wife, and Jesus was born.

Mary cared for Jesus and Joseph with all the love in her heart. She was with Jesus when He was born in the stable and when He died on the cross for our sins. Before He died, Jesus gave us Mary to be our Mother as well.

Prayer to Mother Mary for Mothers

Dear Mother Mary, You are the Mother of Jesus and you are my heavenly mother also. Please bless my mom and all mothers, and help them to feel God's love and joy. Amen.

Dear Mother Mary, pray for us.

SAINT ADRIAN OF NICOMEDIA

Feast Day: September 8
Patron of Correction Officers

Adrian was a member of the palace guard for the Roman Emperor. One day he was presiding over the torture of Christians. Adrian asked them what reward they expected to receive from God. They replied, quoting from Saint Paul's Epistle to the Corinthians, "Eye has not seen, nor ear heard, neither has it entered into the heart of man, the things which God has prepared for them that love Him."

Moved by the joyful courage of these men, Saint Adrian decided to join them, becoming a believer like his wife. The emperor put Adrian in prison and tortured him. His limbs were crushed by anvils and then cut off along with his head. Adrian was martyred around 304 A.D. Today, Saint Adrian of Nicomedia is the patron of correction officers.

Prayer to Saint Adrian for Correction Officers

Glorious Saint Adrian, by guarding the prisoners in your custody, you discovered the key to your own freedom. Help all who work in corrections to be as vigilant as you were in seeking the truth and as valiant as you upon finding it. Bless and safeguard all correction officers. Amen.

Saint Adrian of Nicomedia, pray for us.

SAINT MATTHEW THE APOSTLE

Feast Day: September 21
Patron of Bankers and Accountants

Saint Matthew was a tax collector. One day Jesus walked by and said, "Follow Me." Matthew left his table and taxes to follow the Messiah. Jesus then came to his house for a feast and was criticized by the Pharisees for eating with tax collectors and sinners. Jesus rebuked the Pharisees. He said, "I came not to call the just, but sinners."

Saint Matthew wrote the first Gospel to teach people about Jesus. He preached the new Faith far and wide, and was martyred. Thus Saint Matthew did follow Jesus, all the way to death and to eternal life in heaven.

Because of his work with money as a tax collector, Saint Matthew is recognized today as the patron of bankers.

Prayer to Saint Matthew for Bankers

Dear Saint Matthew, you left everything to follow Jesus when He called you. Please help all bankers and accountants to be honest and trustworthy. Help them to follow Jesus, whatever the cost. Amen.

Saint Matthew, pray for us.

SAINT PIO OF PIETRELCINA

Feast Day: September 23
Patron of All who Suffer

Francesco Forgione was born in Italy, in 1887 and named in honor of Saint Francis. At an early age Francesco felt a deep love for Jesus and Mary, and he became a priest. He joined the Capuchins, a branch of the Franciscan Order, where he was known as Padre Pio. He suffered much, accepting it with praise and thanks to God, trusting that He could use it for the good of others. In 1918, Padre Pio received the stigmata—the wounds of Jesus—in his hands, feet, and side.

Padre Pio listened to confessions of people from all over for many hours every day. Through his prayers, thousands of sick people were healed. Padre Pio deeply loved Saint Michael, his guardian angel, and the souls in Purgatory. Padre Pio died in 1968, and in 2002, Pope John Paul II canonized him as Saint Pio of Pietrelcina!

Prayer to Saint Pio for the Sick

Dear Saint Pio, thank you for offering up your suffering for others. Please pray for all who are sick, especially my family or friends. May God bless and heal them. Amen.

Saint Pio, pray for us.

SAINT VINCENT DE PAUL

Feast Day: September 27
Patron of Prisoners and the Poor

Saint Vincent de Paul was born in France in 1576. He was ordained a priest in 1600. A few years later, he was captured by Turkish pirates and sold into slavery. Saint Vincent escaped to France, where he brought the love and hope of Jesus to prisoners confined to the galleys. He served in a parish near Paris where he started groups to help the poor and forgotten, the sick, and those in need of work. He went through the streets of Paris at night, seeking the children who were left there to die. He founded orders of men and women to help the poor and afflicted, and to bring comfort to all. Saint Vincent de Paul died in 1660.

Prayer to Saint Vincent de Paul for Charity Workers

Dear Saint Vincent, you worked very hard to bring faith, hope, and charity to the poorest of the poor. Please pray that all who serve others will have the same zeal and compassion for the poor that you did. Dear God, through the prayers of Saint Vincent de Paul, please bless all who serve You in the poor and needy. Strengthen them that they may always see You in those they serve. In Jesus' name we pray. Amen.

Saint Vincent de Paul, pray for us.

SAINT GABRIEL THE ARCHANGEL

Feast Day: September 29

Patron of Communications/Postal Workers

Gabriel means *God is my strength*. The Archangel Gabriel was always a messenger of important news. He appeared to the prophet Daniel in the Old Testament. Many years later, he appeared to Zechariah, the husband of Elizabeth and father of John the Baptist. Most importantly, Gabriel announced to Mary that God had chosen her to be the mother of His son, Jesus.

The Archangel Gabriel was very good at sharing God's message with people. He helped them to believe in the good things God wanted to do for them and for the whole world. Gabriel is the patron of postal workers and people who work delivering messages to others. Saint Gabriel will help you understand God's message to you as well!

Prayer to Saint Gabriel for Communication Workers

Dear Saint Gabriel, please bless all who deliver messages via TV, radio, the Internet, or the postal service. Help them bring good news to others. Open our hearts also to hear Our Lord speak to us, and to follow Him. Amen.

Saint Gabriel the Archangel, pray for us.

SAINT MICHAEL THE ARCHANGEL

Feast Day: September 29

Patron of Police Officers and Emergency Personnel

Saint Michael the Archangel is God's most trusted angel, a heavenly messenger who carries out His every command. Michael means *one who is like God.* Saint Michael is a fierce and powerful warrior, protector, and guardian.

Saint Michael is the guardian of Israel and the protector of the Church. When the angel Lucifer—Satan—and his other bad angels started a war in heaven, Michael and his good angels fought them and drove them out of heaven.

Because he is the protector and defender of God's people as well as the angel who brings souls to judgment, Saint Michael the Archangel is recognized today as the patron of police officers and those who keep others safe.

Prayer to Saint Michael for Police Officers

Saint Michael the Archangel, please bless all who work as police officers and guards. Grant them good judgment in keeping the peace, courage in enforcing the law, and honor in giving justice to all. Amen.

Saint Michael the Archangel, pray for us.

SAINT THERESE OF LISIEUX

Feast Day: October 1
Patron of the Missions

Therese Martin was born in France in 1873. She was a happy child who loved Jesus. When her beloved mother died, young Therese became very ill, and she prayed to Mother Mary. Therese saw Mary smile at her and suddenly she was cured! She then became a Carmelite nun. Therese spent her life praying, helping priests, and sacrificing for souls. Loving and trusting in God, as a child, was her "little way" to Jesus. Her favorite saying was, "Love is repaid by love alone." Therese died at the age of 24, whispering, "My God, I love You!" Pope Pius XI canonized Saint Therese in 1925. Two years later, he named her the co-patron of the missions.

Prayer to Saint Therese for the Missions

Dear Saint Therese, you promised to spend your heaven doing good on earth. Please pray for all missionaries that they would always feel God's love and presence as they share His message. Dear God, through the intercession of Saint Therese, please bless all who serve You in other lands. Keep them from all harm and reward them for their faithful service of You. In Jesus' name we pray. Amen.

Saint Therese of Lisieux, pray for us.

SAINT FRANCIS OF ASSISI

Feast Day: October 4

Patron of Animals and All Who Care for the Earth

Saint Francis was born as the son of a wealthy merchant in Assisi in 1182. He loved to sing songs and have fun with his friends. One day, Jesus spoke to Francis from the crucifix in the tiny chapel of San Damiano. He said, "Go, rebuild My Church." Francis fell in love with Jesus. He gave away his rich clothing and wore poor clothes. He cared for the sick and needy. He taught that everything God made, like the sun, the moon, the animals and plants, is good. God wants us to take good care of our earth. Francis gathered many followers and set about spiritually rebuilding the Church.

The pope blessed Saint Francis and his followers. Saint Francis prayed and preached much. He received the wounds of Jesus, and died with the words, "Welcome, Sister Death!"

Prayer to Saint Francis for the Care of our Earth

Dear Saint Francis, you loved Jesus with all your heart. You allowed Him to live His life through you. Please bless all who care for others as you did. Bless those who care for the earth and all God's creatures. Help us to love one another. Amen.

Saint Francis of Assisi, pray for us.

SAINT TERESA OF AVILA

Feast Day: October 15

Patron of People Suffering with Headaches

Saint Teresa was born in Avila, Spain in 1515. When Teresa was only 12 years old, her mother died and her father placed her in a convent. During this time Teresa suffered from painful headaches. She was cured through the prayers of Saint Joseph. Teresa realized that God was calling her to make her convent a holier place, so she reformed the Carmelites. She established 32 monasteries. She also wrote many letters and books which have helped people learn more about prayer and God's love for them.

Saint Teresa died in 1582, was canonized in 1622, and was named the first woman Doctor of the Church in 1970. Saint Teresa of Avila is recognized today as the patron of those suffering with headaches or migraines.

Prayer to Saint Teresa of Avila for Headache Sufferers

Dear Saint Teresa, You followed Jesus Christ, who loved us so much that He chose to be crucified for us. Please pray for all who suffer from headaches, that God will heal them and grant them His peace. Amen.

Saint Teresa of Avila, pray for us.

SAINT GERARD

Feast Day: October 16

Patron of Expectant Mothers and Unborn Children

Saint Gerard was born in Italy in 1726. At the age of 23, he joined the Redemptorist Order. Saint Gerard was obedient, pure, wise, and kind. God gave him gifts of healing and knowing what was in people's hearts.

Saint Gerard spent his life helping the needy and the poor. One day a pregnant mother was concerned about her unborn baby's health. She asked Gerard to pray for her. He did so and she gave birth to a healthy child! God worked many wonders through Saint Gerard. He died at the young age of 29, and was canonized in 1904. Saint Gerard is recognized today as the patron of expectant mothers and of safe delivery of children at birth.

Prayer to Saint Gerard for Mothers

Dear Saint Gerard, please pray for mothers and their unborn children, that God will bless them with the gifts of life, grace, and peace. Dear God, the Giver of Life, through the prayers of Saint Gerard, please help mothers give birth to healthy children who will grow to love You and spread Your love to others. In Jesus' name. Amen.

Saint Gerard, pray for us.

SAINT LUKE THE EVANGELIST

Feast Day: October 18

Patron of Doctors

Saint Luke the Evangelist was born in Antioch, Syria. His parents were Greek. He was a doctor who traveled with Saint Paul on his missionary journeys. Saint Luke ministered with Saint Paul, and helped to heal people who were sick in their bodies and in their souls. In his Epistle to the Colossians, Saint Paul refers to Saint Luke as "the beloved doctor."

Saint Luke wrote the third Gospel as well as the exciting Acts of the Apostles, giving us a history of the infant Church. Historians also think that Saint Luke may have painted some of the earliest icons of Our Lady, including the famous Black Madonna in Poland.

Saint Luke was Saint Paul's faithful companion, and after Paul's death, Luke also died as a martyr in Greece.

Prayer to Saint Luke for Doctors

Dear Saint Luke, you helped to heal many people in body and soul. Help all doctors to do their work carefully and well. Dear God, please help doctors to always treat their patients with compassion and skill. In Jesus' name we pray. Amen.

Saint Luke, pray for us.

SAINT MARTIN DE PORRES

Feast Day: November 3

Patron of Barbers and Interracial Justice

Saint Martin de Porres was born at Lima, Peru, in 1579. His father was a Spanish knight and his mother a freed slave. When he was 15, Martin entered the Dominican Friary at Lima and served as a farm laborer and barber.

He cared for the poor, the sick, and the dying. God endowed Saint Martin with many graces, including humility, gentleness, wisdom, and healing. He opened many orphanages and raised money for children by begging on the streets.

Saint Martin de Porres loved all of God's creation, caring for dogs, cats, and other animals. He was a close friend of Saint Rose of Lima, and he died on November 3, 1639.

Prayer to Saint Martin de Porres for Hairdressers

Dear Saint Martin de Porres, no task was too small for you to perform with great love. Please pray for all barbers and hairdressers. Dear Lord, through the prayers of Saint Martin, bless all hairdressers who seek to make their clients and the world more beautiful. In Jesus' name we pray. Amen.

Saint Martin de Porres, pray for us.

SAINT CHARLES BORROMEO

Feast Day: November 4

Patron of Catechists and Seminarians

Saint Charles was born in 1538 to a noble family in Italy. He was ordained a priest in 1563 and was consecrated bishop of Milan the same year. By wise laws, by gentle kindness, and by his own marvelous example, Saint Charles made his diocese a model for the whole Church. He faithfully prayed and did penance, gave everything he owned to the poor, and set up altars in the streets to bring Mass to the ill.

In 1571, the whole province of Milan suffered from a terrible famine and, later, a plague. Saint Charles worked very hard to help the starving and others who were sick due to the food shortage. He died in 1584.

Prayer to Saint Charles for Seminarians and Catechists

Dear Saint Charles Borromeo, you helped seminarians, priests, and other people to know God better. Please pray for all who teach us about Jesus and our Catholic Faith. Help them to share the love and goodness of Jesus with us, that we might love God and love one another. Amen.

Saint Charles Borromeo, pray for us.

SAINT CECILIA

Feast Day: November 22
Patron of Musicians and Singers

Cecilia, a beautiful and noble Roman maiden, had given herself as a virgin to God. Her parents, however, gave her in marriage to Valerian, a pagan. On their wedding night, Cecilia told her husband that an angel defended her. If he wished to see the angel, he must first be baptized. Valerian heard heavenly music, was baptized and he gave himself to God. His brother also accepted Jesus as His Savior.

The Roman ruler killed Valerian and his brother because they were Christians. Then he commanded Cecilia to be burned in a furnace. But the flames had no power over her, and so the executioner beheaded her. In the year 177, the virgin Saint Cecilia gave back her pure spirit to Christ. Today she is the patron saint of musicians.

Prayer to Saint Cecilia for Musicians

Saint Cecilia, you honored Jesus on earth and you will sing God's praises forever in heaven. Help those who sing or play music to honor God also with their hands and voices. May they compose beautiful music to help other people enjoy and honor God as well. Amen.

Saint Cecilia, pray for us.

SAINT CATHERINE OF ALEXANDRIA

Feast Day: November 25

Patron of Secretaries

Saint Catherine was a noble Catholic virgin of Alexandria, Egypt. At the age of 18, she told the emperor that he was wrong to persecute Christians. He sent 50 pagan philosophers to argue with her, but Catherine converted them! The emperor ordered Catherine to be imprisoned and scourged. In prison Catherine converted the emperor's wife and 200 of his soldiers. The emperor became very angry when he heard this. He ordered Catherine to be executed on a spiked wheel. It shattered at her touch, and he beheaded Catherine in 305 AD.

Devotion to Saint Catherine spread during the Crusades. Students, teachers, and others asked for her patronage.

Prayer to Saint Catherine for Secretaries

Glorious Saint Catherine, virgin and martyr, you spoke tirelessly of God to all who would listen, neither breaking nor turning away from Him even though tortured. Inspire, by your holy example, all who work serving others as secretaries. May their commitment to Jesus, who is the Way, the Truth, and the Life, be total and true. Amen.

Saint Catherine of Alexandria, pray for us.

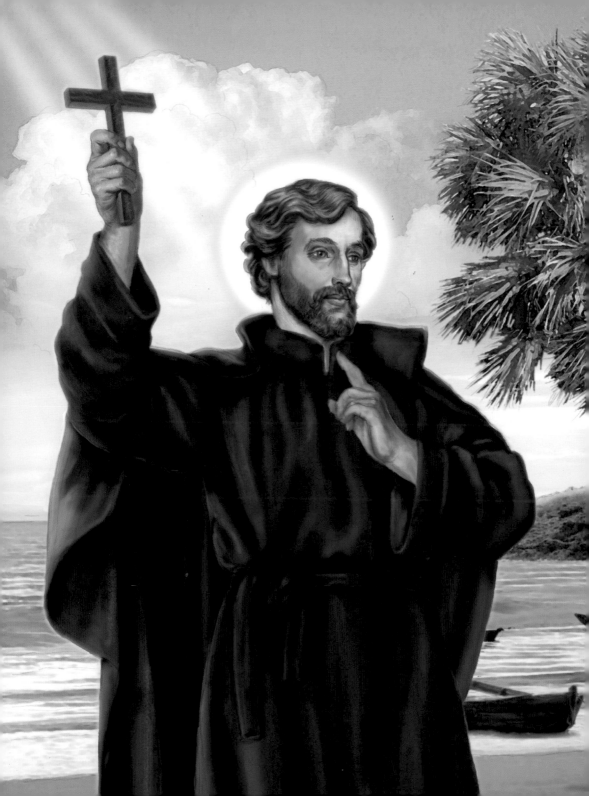

SAINT FRANCIS XAVIER

Feast Day: December 3
Patron of Missionaries

Saint Francis Xavier was born to noble parents in Spain in 1506. He enjoyed sports and school. He attended the University of Paris where he met Saint Ignatius of Loyola. Ignatius helped Francis give himself to Jesus Christ. Francis and some companions helped Saint Ignatius establish the Society of Jesus—*the Jesuits*—and he was ordained a priest in 1537. He sailed to India and baptized thousands of people from there to Japan. Saint Francis set out for China, and died within sight of that great country in 1552. Saint Francis Xavier is considered the greatest missionary since Saint Paul. In 1904, Pope Saint Pius X proclaimed him the patron of all foreign missions.

Prayer to Saint Francis Xavier for Missionaries

Dear Saint Francis Xavier, God called you to preach the Gospel to the peoples of India and Asia. Please pray for all those who bring God's good news to people in far away lands. Dear God, through the prayers of Your servant Saint Francis Xavier, help us to feel Your love burning in our hearts. Help us to be not afraid to speak of You to all we meet. In Jesus' name. Amen.

Saint Francis Xavier, pray for us.

SAINT BARBARA

Feast Day: December 4
Patron of Builders and Architects

Saint Barbara was born in the 3rd century. Her pagan father hid her in a lonely tower. While he was away, Barbara had builders install a third window to honor the Holy Trinity.

When her father saw what she had done, he dragged her to the Roman governor. The governor ordered his soldiers to torture Barbara and cut off her head. Barbara held on to her faith in Jesus, and in a rage, her father drew his sword and beheaded her himself. On his way home he was struck and killed by a flash of lightning. Saint Barbara is honored as the patron of architects, because of her imprisonment in the tower.

Prayer to Saint Barbara for Architects

Dear Saint Barbara, your great love for the Holy Trinity moved you to witness to God through architecture. By preparing a place for Christ in your heart, you won a place for yourself in the house of your Heavenly Father.

Dear God, through the prayers of Saint Barbara, please bless all architects and builders who continue Your work of creation. In Jesus' name. Amen.

Saint Barbara, pray for us.

SAINT NICHOLAS
Feast Day: December 6
Patron of Children and Sailors

Saint Nicholas was born in a province of Asia Minor during the third century. His parents were devout Christians and extremely wealthy. They died while Nicholas was still young. He gave all his money to help the poor, the sick, and children in need. He often helped others in secret. Nicholas was sent to live in a monastery and became one of the youngest priests ever.

Nicholas dedicated his life to serving God and others. In the early part of the fourth century he was made Bishop of Myra. It was said that he was not just able to nurse sick children back to health—he could raise them from the dead! Saint Nicholas died in 342 A.D. and is recognized as the protector and patron of all children and of sailors.

Prayer to Saint Nicholas for Children and Sailors

Dear Saint Nicholas, please bless all children and help them to know and love Jesus. You once appeared to sailors during a great storm and helped them to float safely into port. Please bless all sailors with grace and peace. Amen.

Saint Nicholas, pray for us.

SAINT LUCY

Feast Day: December 13
Patron of Those with Eye Ailments

Saint Lucy was born to a rich family in Sicily around the year 283. Lucy gave herself to Jesus as His special bride at an early age. Not knowing this, her mother promised Lucy in marriage to a young pagan man named Paschasius. Paschasius told the governor that Lucy was a Christian. The governor ordered his guards to take out her eyes. God miraculously restored Lucy's eyesight, and the governor ordered his guards to set a fire around her. Again, God saved her. Finally, the guards killed Lucy with a dagger.

In Sicily and Italy, there is a story that Saint Lucy travels door to door in a donkey-drawn wagon with gifts for children on her feast day. That is why she is also the patron of salespeople.

Prayer to Saint Lucy for Those with Eye Ailments

Dear Saint Lucy, you brightened the lives of those around you by sharing good things with others. Please pray for all who suffer with eye ailments and blindness. Through your prayers, may God give them perfect vision. May they use their eyes for His greater honor and glory. Amen.

Saint Lucy, pray for us.

SAINT JOHN THE APOSTLE

Feast Day: December 27
Patron of Booksellers

Jesus called John at a very young age to follow Him and become an Apostle. Saint John stood faithfully with Mary by Jesus as He hung on the Cross. Jesus in turn gave His Mother to John, who took her into his home. During the era of the new Church, Saint John preached in Jerusalem and Ephesus. He later wrote a Gospel and three Epistles.

The emperor tried to kill John in boiling oil, but God delivered him. Saint John wrote the Book of Revelation and died in the year 100. Saint John is recognized today as the patron of book sellers, art dealers, and printers.

Prayer to Saint John for Booksellers

Dear Saint John, you loved Jesus so much in your life that you are called the beloved apostle. Jesus entrusted His Mother to you as your Mother. Through your words and works, you have taught us how to love God. Bless all who work in printing and publishing, and help them to also draw people to God as they serve Him through their work. Amen.

Saint John the Apostle, pray for us.

PRAYER TO ALL PATRON SAINTS

Dear Saints in heaven, we praise God today for the gift you are to Him and to us. We thank God for giving each of you such big hearts, true hearts, and generous hearts. You did not think of yourselves in this life, but how you could serve God and others. You believed in and received God's great love, the love of His Holy Spirit, into your hearts. Your hearts burn with the fire of the Sacred Heart of Jesus and the purity of the Immaculate Heart of Mary.

Like Our Mother Mary, Queen of all Saints, you said to God, "Let it be done unto me according to Thy Word!" You gave all you had to Our Lord, and you did not count the cost. Many of you gave your lives as martyrs—witnesses of Jesus and His love. You were willing to choose death rather than sin.

By your lives, you teach us to pray, hope, and not to worry. You show us that if we are what we should be, we will set the world ablaze! You teach us to be instruments of God's peace, because it is no longer we who live, but Christ Jesus who lives in us. You teach us that our hearts are made for God, and we will not be happy until we rest in Him. You teach us to go out into the deep, and to lower our nets for a catch. You call us to do something beautiful for God. You remind us that in the end, the greatest of these is love.

Help us then, dear Saints of God, to feel the love of Jesus in our hearts. Help us to know and love God a little more each day. Please pray that God will give us the gift of a servant heart, that we will be ready and willing to serve others, especially those who are poor, lonely, and forgotten. Help us love Jesus and Mary, and to put all our trust in God, our dearest Father in heaven. Amen.